I'm a Stegosaurus

my dinosaur adventure

CHERRY LAKE PRESS

Published in the United States of America by Cherry Lake Publishing
Ann Arbor, Michigan
www.cherrylakepublishing.com

Reading Adviser: Marla Conn, MS, Ed., Literacy specialist, Read-Ability, Inc.
Content Adviser: Kierstin Rosenbach, Ph.D. Candidate, Vertebrate Paleontology, University of Michigan
Book Designer: Jennifer Wahi
Illustrator: Jeff Bane

Photo Credits: © Linda Bucklin/Shutterstock.com, 5; © Catmando/Shutterstock.com, 7; © Karel Bartik/
Shutterstock.com, 9; © EddieCloud/Shutterstock.com, 11; © Warpaint/Shutterstock.com, 13; © Maris Grunskis/
Shutterstock.com, 15; © Daniel Eskridge/Shutterstock.com, 17; © Evgeniia Shikhaleeva/Shutterstock.com, 19;
© Paul Barron/Shutterstock.com, 21; © Catmando/Shutterstock.com, 23; Cover, 2-3, 10, 18, 22, 24, Jeff Bane

Library of Congress Cataloging-in-Publication Data

Names: Nelson, Jake, author. | Bane, Jeff, 1957- illustrator.
Title: I'm a stegosaurus / Jake Nelson; illustrator, Jeff Bane.
Description: Ann Arbor, Michigan: Cherry Lake Publishing, [2021] | Series:
   My dinosaur adventure | Includes index. | Audience: Grades K-1
Identifiers: LCCN 2020002501 (print) | LCCN 2020002502 (ebook) | ISBN
   9781534168510 (hardcover) | ISBN 9781534170193 (paperback) | ISBN
   9781534172036 (pdf) | ISBN 9781534173873 (ebook)
Subjects: LCSH: Stegosaurus--Juvenile literature.
Classification: LCC QE862.O65 N45 2021 (print) | LCC QE862.O65 (ebook) |
   DDC 567.915/3--dc23
LC record available at https://lccn.loc.gov/2020002501
LC ebook record available at https://lccn.loc.gov/2020002502

Printed in the United States of America
Corporate Graphics

About the author: Jake Nelson was born and raised in Minnesota, where he enjoys everything from watching the Twins at Target Field to strolling along the shore of Lake Superior. He writes books, blogs, and content for the web.

About the illustrator: Jeff Bane and his two business partners own a studio along the American River in Folsom, California, home of the 1849 Gold Rush. When Jeff's not sketching or illustrating for clients, he's either swimming or kayaking in the river to relax.

Hi there!
I'm a Stegosaurus.

I lived about 150 million years ago.

This was called the **Mesozoic era**.

I am around 30 feet (9 meters) long.

I weigh about as much as six hippos!

Can you name another herbivore?

I am an **herbivore**. I eat plants.

Other dinosaurs are **carnivores**. They eat other dinosaurs.

I have plates on my back.
I have spikes on my tail.

My tail spikes can be up to
3 feet (1 m) long.

My plates and spikes keep **predators** away.

I do not want to be eaten!

My plates may have just been for looks.

They are pretty cool!

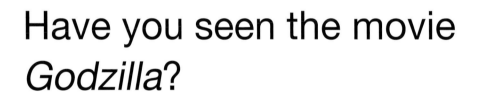

What other creatures inspired *Godzilla*?

Have you seen the movie *Godzilla*?

I was one of the dinosaurs it is based on.

Paleontologists are still studying my **fossils**.

There is more to discover!

What makes you unique?

One thing is for sure.

I am one special dinosaur.

glossary

carnivores (KAHR-nuh-vorz) creatures that only eat other living things, like animals or bugs

fossils (FAH-suhlz) bones that turned to stone in the ground

herbivore (HUR-buh-vor) a creature that only eats plants, like grass and leaves

Mesozoic era (mez-uh-ZOH-ik ER-uh) the period of time when dinosaurs lived on Earth, between 245 million and 66 million years ago

paleontologists (pay-lee-uhn-TAH-luh-jists) scientists who study dinosaurs

predators (PRED-uh-turz) creatures that hunt and eat other creatures

index